Visvavictor: Kanima Akiyor Kainat

Abhijit Naskar is the 21st century Neuroscientist and Poet who has been serving at the forefront of humankind's struggle against hate, intolerance, bigotry and fanaticism.

# Visvavictor

## KANIMA AKIYOR KAINAT

ABHIJIT
NASKAR

Also by Abhijit Naskar

The Art of Neuroscience in Everything
Your Own Neuron: A Tour of Your Psychic Brain
The God Parasite: Revelation of Neuroscience
The Spirituality Engine
Love Sutra: The Neuroscientific Manual of Love
Homo: A Brief History of Consciousness
Neurosutra: The Abhijit Naskar Collection
Autobiography of God: Biopsy of A Cognitive Reality
Biopsy of Religions: Neuroanalysis towards Universal
Tolerance
Prescription: Treating India's Soul
What is Mind?
In Search of Divinity: Journey to The Kingdom of Conscience
Love, God & Neurons: Memoir of a scientist who found
himself by getting lost
The Islamophobic Civilization: Voyage of Acceptance
Neurons of Jesus: Mind of A Teacher, Spouse & Thinker
Neurons, Oxygen & Nanak
The Education Decree
Principia Humanitas
The Krishna Cancer
Rowdy Buddha: The First Sapiens
We Are All Black: A Treatise on Racism
The Bengal Tigress: A Treatise on Gender Equality
Either Civilized or Phobic: A Treatise on Homosexuality
Wise Mating: A Treatise on Monogamy
Illusion of Religion: A Treatise on Religious
Fundamentalism
The Film Testament
Human Making is Our Mission: A Treatise on Parenting
I Am The Thread: My Mission
7 Billion Gods: Humans Above All
Lord is My Sheep: Gospel of Human
Morality Absolute
A Push in Perception
Let The Poor Be Your God
Conscience over Nonsense
Saint of The Sapiens
Time to Save Medicine
Fabric of Humanity
Build Bridges not Walls: In the name of Americana
The Constitution of The United Peoples of Earth

Lives to Serve Before I Sleep
When Humans Unite: Making A World Without Borders
All For Acceptance
Monk Meets World
Mission Reality
Citizens of Peace: Beyond The Savagery of Sovereignty
Operation Justice: To Make A Society That Needs No Law
See No Gender
The Gospel of Technology
Every Generation Needs Caretakers: The Gospel of
Patriotism
Aşkanjali: The Sufi Sermon
Mad About Humans: World Maker's Almanac
Revolution Indomable
When Call The People: My World My Responsibility
No Foreigner Only Family
Hurricane Humans: Give me accountability, I'll give you
peace
Ain't Enough to Look Human
Servitude is Sanctitude
Time To End Democracy: The Meritocratic Manifesto
I Vicdansaadet Speaking: No Rest Till The World is Lifted
Boldly Comes Justice: Sentient not Silent
Good Scientist: When Science and Service Combine
Sleepless for Society
Neden Türk: The Gospel of Secularism
Martyr Meets World: To Solve The Hard Problem of
Inhumanity
The Shape of A Human: Our America Their America
When Veins Ignite: Either Integration or Degradation
Heart Force One: Need No Gun to Defend Society
Solo Standing on Guard: Life Before Law
Generation Corazon: Nationalism is Terrorism
Mucize Insan: When The World is Family
Hometown Human: To Live For Soil and Society
Girl Over God: The Novel
Gente Mente Adelante: Prejudice Conquered is World
Conquered
Earthquakin' Egalitarian: I Die Everyday So Your Children
Can Live
Giants in Jeans: 100 Sonnets of United Earth
Vatican Virus: The Forbidden Fiction (Abi Naskar
Adventures Book 2)
Karadeniz Chronicle: The Novel (Abi Naskar Adventures

# DEDICATION

*For my Türkiye – without you,*
*there would be no "Naskar the Poet".*

# CONTENTS

# Part 1

14

## Sonnet 1144

Istanbul to Alpha Centauri,
Cosmos courses in my corpuscles.
Religion, nation, stuff it all,
Benevolence makes the world livable.

Din, dünya, milliyet falan,
hiç umurumda değil.
Sen mutlu ol - bana yeter.
Scripture, constitution, god, government,
Nothing matters to me, except behavior.

The greatest iftar is
to break the fast of apathy,
with the feast of affection.
Sin humano no hay dios,
Where there is no kindness
there is no divine intervention.

Sapiens intervention is divine intervention,
There is nothing higher or more mighty.
When we are obliterated in lifting the fallen,
That's the living manifestation of the almighty.

Part 2

## Sonnet 1145

19

You are my Mecca,
You are my Bethlehem,
You are my El Dorada,
You are my Washington.

Istanbul to Alpha Centauri,
Tu sonrisa es mi cura.
California to Kanyakumari,
Sen gülünce ben fakira.

Buenos Aires to Brasilia,
Tu bienestar es mi mañana.
To love and lift is my prime directive,
Lucha por igualdad es la lucha divina.

Sonnet 1146

**Manhood Diaries**
(The Sonnet)


Onun için cennet ol, cehennem değil.
Vicdanlı bir adam ol, hayvan değil.
Sé una bendición para ella, no una maldición.
Onun yaralarına ilacı ol, tuz değil.

Be her paradise, not prison.
Be her man, not master.
Be a miracle to her maladies.
Be her crown, not custard.

There is no alpha male and beta male,
There is only man and baboon.
Decency defines a man's character,
Not the virility of his heirloom.

Partner on the streets,
Slave between the sheets,
That's what a real man is.
Undaunted in danger,
Uncompromising in calamity,
That's what a real human is.

## Sonnet 1147

Only way to grow together as a couple,
is to nourish each other's individual growth.
Only way to grow together as a society,
is to empower each other's personal growth.

Learn from Manu, Majnun, Vyas and M.A.S.H,
Absorb all good like an eager sponge.
Tradition of tribe has outstayed its welcome,
Now outgrow the fences across fearful hunch.

Na desi, na videsi,
Banna hai to bano visvadesi.
Bohot aye despar marnevaale,
Des ke par chalo sudhare
insani zindagi.

Ni local, ni extranjero,
Simplemente seamos humano.
Más allá de la patria,
más allá de la muerte,
Vivamos como un planeta pueblo.

Ni obediente, ni opresivo -
Luchando por igualdad seremos humano.

23

# Part 3

24

Dulce mente, dulce mundo -
Basta de brutalidad,
Es hora de ser humano!
Los animales pueden caer en el odio,
Soy humano - me voy enamorando!

Kanıma akıyor tüm kâinat,
Artık benim kâinat sensin.
Zor geliyor medeniyet falan,
Artık tek medeniyetim sensin.

Ain't no civilization without civilians,
Ain't no civilian without civic duty.
The greatest country on earth, is earth -
Belief is your right, not bigotry.

Sonnet 1148

## DEI Sonnet

I call it curiosity,
You call it science.
I call it integrity,
You call it defiance.
I call it contemplation,
You call it philosophy.
I call it accountability,
You call it sociology.
I call it correction,
You call it revolution.
I call it existence,
You call it inclusion.
All I see is humans
finally living a human life.
You with your brainy fancy
philosophize it as DEI.

Sonnet 1149

## Get Well Soon
(The Sonnet)


Upon absorbing all cultures into my blood,
I realize, the supreme culture is love.
Upon studying all scriptures as my own,
I realize, the supreme gospel is love.
Even after speaking six languages,
I say, the supreme language is love.
Upon observing all political ideologies,
I say, only ideal worth submission is love.
Unfolding the neural underpinnings of behavior,
I realize, seed of civilization is love.
Unraveling the cellular mysteries of life,
I realize, existence oughta be a record of love.
Tiny-brained know-it-alls will still yell,
their culture beats all, like some tipsy loon.
To which all I can say is - get well soon!


Now more than ever the hateful, intolerant, separatist bigots need our help, for they are ill, terribly ill. They are suffering from a condition, I call, Clinical Culturitis. So next time you see one, offer them a flower, and say - get well soon!

# Part 4

Sonnet 1150

## First Language
(The Sonnet)


English is my second language,
My first language is love.
Neuroscience is my second sense,
My first sense is love.

Theology is my second faith,
My first faith is interfaith.
Philosophy is my second nature,
My first nature is to assimilate.

Analog is my second passion,
My first passion is dialogue.
Law is my second task, my first,
Is taking beings out of the bog.

All labels are second labels,
Our native label is human.
All tradition is second tradition,
Earth's native tradition is compassion.

## Sonnet 1151

32

The best use of language
is to surpass the language.
The best use of culture
is to surpass all culture.
The best use of religion
is to surpass religion.
The best use of politics
is to surpass politics.
The best use of law
is to surpass all legality.
The best use of philosophy
is to surpass philosophy.
The best use of time
is to surpass all time.
The best use of life
is to expand into light.

## Sonnet 1152

In Korea, I am Ingan -
In Turkiye, I am Insan.
In Latam, Soy Humano -
In North America, I'm Human.

In hindi, I am Khichdi*,
A *hodge-podge of cultures,
Few have the mind to stomach,
while tribals feel perturbed.

Life is love, love is life -
all other existence is null and void.
World is love, love is the world** -
all other paradigm is poison voyage.

**Originally the line came to me in Korean, as "세상은 사랑, 사랑은 세상 (sesan-eun salang, salan-eun sesang)". If you love a culture, you gotta do something for that culture. It doesn't matter whether you are born in that culture - the real question is, what have you done for that culture? That's how we build an integrated society - or better yet, that's how we build a unified world. And my soldiers are to be the forerunners of that unified world - my soldiers are to be the forebearers of unification.

Part 5

## Sonnet 1153

# Verb Over Noun
### (The Sonnet)

I do the best of my writing,
When I don't feel like a writer.
I create the best of my philosophy,
When I don't feel like a philosopher.
I write the best of my poetry,
When I don't deem myself a poet.
I publish the best of my science,
Walking just a pilgrim of knowledge.
Labels we hold dear often hold us captive,
So do not take the acronym for the act.
Designations can't contain the designated,
Move past the noun and let the verb enact.

## Sonnet 1154

Hate only keeps traveling round the world,
Until one person chooses to break the cycle.
War only keeps migrating border to border,
Until one nation chooses to break the cycle.

Our ancestors handed us hate as heritage,
Like good little apes we embraced it as honor.
Never for a moment we paused to ponder,
How one stupid prejudice leads to another!

We have the capacity to conquer the stars,
Yet we've chained ourselves to the graveyard.
In the guise of prehistoric patriotism,
Apes made a paradigm out of hate and hurt.

Such paradigm belongs in bin -
it's time, the cycle breaks.
Bomb the world with music,
pizza and poetry you idiots,
not Semtex, C4 and RDX.

As the tail on our back disappeared as we no longer had any use for it, nuclear weapons will also disappear once we realize, we no longer have any need for them. But no matter how much we daydream, it will never happen as some sort of grand geopolitical gesture of international collaboration - somebody has to take the first step - one nuclear-capable state has to take that first leap of bold faith and naive trust! The question is, who will it be? The first nuclear nation to abandon its nuclear weapons, will be the First Peacemaking Nation of Earth - and their head of state, the First Peacemaker.

# Part 6

42

## Sonnet 1155

Analyze like a scientist,
plot like a politician,
execute like a soldier.
Don't expose your faculties,
unless absolutely necessary -
Better sober pretending drunk,
than drunk pretending sober.

Never blabber about your plans,
Speak of plans as little as possible.
It's not about maintaining secrecy,
It's about drawing less attention,
till you achieve the impossible.

Make friends with the night,
Soon dawn will break as your aid.
Those who crave dawn all night long,
Spend their life in the darkest grave.

Discreetly do your due diligence,
Speak up when you're spoken down to.
Work your plan, don't publicize it -
Your work will stir up noise,
you don't need to.

## Sonnet 1156

Those who love you, will love you
despite your occasional cockups.
Those who hate you, will hate you
despite your evident triumphs.

Muerte por una misión
es la vida suprema.
Vivir sin una visión
es la muerte vergonzosa.

Sight up - might up - light up!
Denounce the shore and sail the sea!
Draw electricity from your spinal cord,
One brain can make or break society.

Mind is the moment, moment is space -
Wake up in the space of moment -
Time will submit to you,
and make you omnipresent.

When you are present,
present is a gift -
Oblivious to the present,
present starts to drift.

Cameras are supposed to help you relive a moment, but if you never live the moment in the first place, because you are too busy taking pictures, how will you relive it!

At some point in life you lose interest in new devices, new clothes, new trends - and it dawns on you, what's really important in life, is people. That's when you really start living. And the tragedy is, most people come to this realization when one foot is already in the grave. So, know the value of people, my friend - the sooner you do, the sooner you'll know life.

Part 7

## Sonnet 1157

Like junk food there is something I call junk tech,
where you clutter your life with unnecessary gadgets.
More cluttered the life, more cluttered the mind -
and a mind cluttered is a mind wrecked.

But the picture is not black and white as it seems -
When technology does good, credit goes to humans -
When technology screws up, blame goes to technology.
That's why I don't advocate for a world without AI,
I call for a world where AI is used responsibly.

Drones can be used to plant a forest,
Drones can be used to bomb a school.
Drones don't know right from wrong,
It's the d**k flying 'em causes all doom.

Blame the d**k, not the drone,
Blame the consumer, not the code.
Since the consumer is none but us,
Responsible consumerism is a crucial
part of civic duty - that's how
we transform our global abode.

## Sonnet 1158

It's been two hundred thousand years,
since we developed the face of human.
Question is, how many more millennia,
till we develop the heart of human!

We are still stuck in a battle of lingo,
We prioritize description over descripted.
We take the menu for the meal,
We still can't bear a life unscripted.

So we look for handbooks here and there -
In the process we get trapped in prejudice.
The chaos of it all scares us to death -
That fear keeps us falling for tricks.

Some trick us with talk of magic,
Others trick us with intellect.
Either way we remain ever so afraid,
Never to be our own President elect.

# Part 8

52

Although there is no place for superstitious fantasies in my life, I have always made allowance for one particular innocent fantasy (those who've studied the origin of Naskar would know why). It is that, my late teacher is somehow looking after me. Now you don't have to go all big and intellectual to remind me that it's all in my mind. Believe you me, nobody knows what's in the mind, what's not, better than a brain scientist. The scientist in me knows it's all in my mind, yet the child in me wants to believe. And so long as that belief is not jeopardizing my faculties - far from it, it actually empowers them - no intellectual is righteous enough to command me to abandon my belief as it is not rooted in evidence.

You see, the problem is not that we believe in a lot of weird stuff, the problem is that often we end up confusing our belief with reality. Keep your belief if you need, no matter how illogical it is, but always be observant of your belief. Be the believer as well as the observer of the believer. In your mind be a child as well as the guardian of the child. Allow yourself some fantasy if it's not doing any harm, but never let it run amok.

Let me put it to you another way - a little bit of fantasy actually enhances your mental faculties. Which means, just like there is such a thing as too much fantasy, there is also such a thing as too much logic. Apply logic where logic is needed, permit fantasy where fantasy does good. Learn to be flexible, learn to be human.

In simple words, you gotta be mindful of your rationality as well as your fantasies. Being mindful doesn't mean being open to the supernatural, being mindful means being open to the natural - being mindful means being present in the present.

I tell you as a Neuroscientist - fantasy is a human right, and when practiced with caution, it enhances mental health, as well as creativity.

Fantasy is a mental marvel, but the problem is, fantasies have a tendency to take over - at which point innocent fantasy becomes lethal superstition - which then is exploited by cultish institutions such as the Vatican for sectarian gains.

Let me elaborate.

The Vatican has been sending out missionaries across the world not to help the poor, but to convert the poor, in exchange for charity. In this respect, empirically speaking, the only religion that has been practicing the tradition of actual selfless service religiously, is Sikhism. Till this day Sikh langars or soup-kitchens across the world feed millions of people regularly, no matter their status, faith or ethnicity, without asking for anything in return. Religious charity in exchange for religious conversion is the most sacrilegious act of all. In the end, it has nothing to do with religion, and everything to do with service. Either serve or don't, there is no spreading the word. Spread good acts, not good news.

That's how we evolve from an animal species to a human species.

Evolution doesn't happen based on evidence, evolution is an act of accident. And when we choose the accidental act of kindness over the evolutionary certainty of cruelty, only then can we set in motion a civilized paradigm where kindness is the norm, not cruelty, and cruelty is the anomaly, not kindness.

56

**Part 9**

## Soneto de Idiota

Yo no nací latino,
¡aún así me aceptarás,
como tu gente propia!
Mi corazón, alma, todo roto,
¿aceptarás las piezas como precio,
por un lugar pequeño en tu familia?
Me cuesta hablar español,
todavía hay mucho que escribo.
Poesía sólo necesita un buen corazón,
ni impecable gramática, ni vocabulario.
Soy local porque soy responsable -
Cada pueblo mi pueblo, mi humanidad insiste.
Got no past no future, el idiota stands at your door,
And I ask you again, ¿me tomarás como tu gente?

Every people is my people - heart trumps all nationality - heart trumps state. State is a filthy word, a revolting reminder of animality.

However, one thing we mustn't overlook either - at least in democracy people choose their own fool, which is far from civilized, since the election itself is not based on merit but charisma - still it is a step towards a civilized future, that is, a meritocratic future - but this very possibility is nonexistent in a society run by monarchy, where any moronic lowlife can be declared head of state based on bloodline, just like the good old medieval days.

Sonnet 1159

## Beyond King and Crumpet
(Uncoronation Sonnet)


There's not one but two UKs -
one is United Kingdom,
where animals worship a king,
another is United Kin-dom,
where humans live as kin.

Storm's coming! Huts and homes
of the humble will thrive,
while castles and palaces
of thieves will crumble.
Either we are explorers
of equality and dignity, or
we are crown worshipping animal.

Putting all kings and queens to bed,
Citizens must come out and work the soil.
Enough chasing the parade of dead meat,
March your own parade, tackling turmoil!

Crown, cross and rigid constitution,
Mindlessness has taken many a form.
Beyond the fetish of king and crumpet,
Beckon the rays of an honorable dawn.

62

# Part 10

When a philandering ass is declared head of state, and the other woman sleeps her way to the throne, it's not a moment of national pride, it's an outlandish declaration of national pestilence.

Better britain begins with a better brit, an inclusive brit, a decolonized brit - a brit who knows no king and queen - a brit who celebrates no tomfoolery of coronation - a brit who knows but one race, the human race - a brit who knows but one religion, love - a brit who knows but one tradition, integration.

However, I must make one thing clear. England is not the only country with problems - every country has them.

If you want to move to a country where there is no social issue, you'd have to move to a different planet. If it's not monarchy, it's racism - if it's not racism, it's fundamentalism - if it's not fundamentalism, it's nationalism. No country is born great, it has to be made great. No planet is born human, it has to be made human, by the conscientious intervention of backbone-primed humans.

No matter where you live on earth, every society has its own troubles. The only way to break free from troubles is to charge at them like a headstrong hurricane. Remember, there is no storm more purifying than a backbone-primed human being.

And we are not going to achieve this by fighting over ideologies. We gotta look past ideology - or to be specific, we gotta look past terminology.

Ideology is nothing but a bunch of fancy terms. And when you are human enough to outgrow the pettiness of terms, only then shall you have the insight to do something meaningful in your society. Otherwise, you shall be ever stuck in the narcissistic battle of terminologies, like the rest of the egotistical bunch of intellectual morons.

And how will you know, you have outgrown all childish nonsense of ideological intellectualism - when you no longer crave to use fancy words in conversations - when you no longer lust after proving your intellectual superiority by dropping linguistic bombs ever so often.

However, let me put it in a lingo that I know, you are craving to hear.

The terms we use tell a lot about our intentions, because terminologies are linguistic markers of our subconscious tendencies. For example, the term geopolitics is actually code for global indifference.

Let me elaborate.

We rarely use the term family politics, right!

You know why?

Because it's too damn personal.

What's personal cannot be politicized, what's politicized cannot be personal. If the world were personal to us like our family, there wouldn't be any clash of ideology in society.

Simple words reflect simple soul, and simple soul makes the greatest reformer. And in the heart of the reformer, there is no place for ideological allegiance.

Part 11

Ruhunda aşkı göremiyorsa,
Kanında kâinatı bulamıyorsa,
Lanet olsun bu canavar ruhuna,
Kahretsin bu hayvanın kanına!

Benevolence in bone marrow,
Conscience in corpuscles,
Answer the dare of coward hate,
Trudging all ancient rage 'n rubble.

In a reality crippled by cruelty,
Be the gateway to an alternate reality.
In a dimension reeking of division,
Be the new specimen of united humanity.

How do we erase phobia from the world? First make a name for yourself, then associate that name to everything the world is ignorantly afraid of. In a pavlovian world where rating-hungry separatist media has conditioned the people to subconsciously relate every act of terror to a specific community, use your life to decondition the world - stand as the first human who is not afraid of humankind. That's why I say - I am a muslim poet, a humanitarian scientist, a latin lover, and an advaitin monk - I am an alternate dimension - an immeasurable dimension - where human oneness takes preference over animal separateness.

## Sonnet 1160

Presence of oneness doesn't
mean absence of differences,
Presence of oneness means
absence of intolerance.

Presence of justice doesn't
mean absence of injustice,
Presence of justice means
absence of indifference.

Presence of reason doesn't
mean absence of fantasy,
Presence of reason means
absence of superstition.

Just because I don't believe in the same fantasies you believe in, doesn't mean I'll stop standing by you. So long as there is kindness in your heart, you'll have a friend in me.

Besides, let me tell you a secret of cognition. Even the most logical of minds holds some sort of fantasy, with or without being aware of it. So, instead of focusing on our innocent fantasies, let's focus on what we are good at.

You do something best,
I do something best -
when we come together,
we make a better society.
But you suck at something,
I suck at something -
and when we are busy picking
on each other's shortcomings,
we have a sucker for society.

The problem is, so far we have never actually, genuinely prioritized transformation over tradition. Either we force others to integrate into our way of life, or we bar them from our community altogether. Integration has never been our objective - our true objective has always been the exclusive welfare and triumph of our own tribe. Unless this primeval tendency is overwhelmed by a genuine human desire for collective growth and universal assimilation, there is no question of peace.

# Part 12

## Sonnet 1161

### Visvavictor Sonnet

I am not a poet,
I am a paradigm.
I am no religionist,
But the source divine.
More than a scientist,
I'm a compass to science.
I am not a philosopher,
But a purposeful alliance.
I am not some legal giant,
But a valley of lawless order.
Transcending Sieg Heil and Star Spangled Banner,
I am the Visva (world), I am the Victor.

## Sonnet 1162

Some shout Sieg Heil,
Some shout Jai Hind.
Some Star Spangled Banner,
Others God save the fiend.

Only the language differs,
Jungliness remains the same.
Even in an integrating world,
Some maintain the habits lame.

Once upon a time,
they might have had some value.
Today they are just anachronism,
Kept alive by apes without clue.

If you are still enraged,
how dare I compare
Sieg Heil with the rest!
Study the history unvarnished -
behind every tribal salute
you'll find a holocaust equivalent.

# Part 13

Sociologically speaking, American democracy is the perfect specimen of a dysfunctional democracy. When a supremacist president incites racist hate and terrorist violence, out of bigotry and boneheadedness, his stoneage supporters consider it a matter of pride, but when an egalitarian president so much as mispronounces a few words due to his medical stammer, he is deemed incompetent by those people. Which only goes to show, no matter how much a nation tries to right the wrongs of its inhuman origin, there will always be some people who'd consider those inhumanities as their proud heritage, and would go to any length to maintain those customs and beliefs as such. And this is not an American phenomenon, it's a worldwide phenomenon - and everywhere it manifests under the same banner of tradition, heritage and nationalism.

That is why I say to you - until we oust every last trace of nationalism from every corner of this world, we shall never in a million years have a genuinely integrated and upward-moving society. Either nationalism or humanity, you cannot have both - either borders or peace, you cannot have both - either guns or children, you cannot have both - either heritage or history, you cannot have both.

If history comes as a blow to your heritage, then by all means, live in your bubble - but do so as a prehistoric ape disconnected from the civilizing world. You cannot call yourself a civilized human and at the same time refuse to acknowledge human suffering. Your uncivilization may be your prerogative, but before you turn that uncivilization into the norm, you shall find a hundred MLKs, Baldwins, Mayas and Naskars standing as obstacle to your insanity.

# Part 14

## Sonnet 1163

We gotta outgrow all tribes,
all nazi counterparts.
All nationalism is nazism -
Outgrow all that keep us apart.

It's a new world we gotta build -
Founded on love, tempered by reason.
If we must keep the borders,
let's keep them as external necessity,
not as internal prison.

Basta de mi gente tu gente -
somos todos una gente.
Yeter ya, benim millet,
senin millet falan -
bütün dünya bir millet.

Enough with my people your people -
it's all just one people.

## Sonnet 1164

Soy vivo cuando somos vivos -
Existence actually means coexistence.
I live when we live, I exist when we exist -
Togetherness is only true existence.

Tomorrow is togetherness -
No togetherness, no tomorrow.
Separation is the end of time.
Time is togetherness -
togetherness tomorrow!

Heart is what makes time,
Heart is what breaks time.
Hate is a stain on heart,
Hate is a stain on time.

Hate is a desecration of space-time.
Hate is degradation of human mind.

# Jai Ho
## (Sonnet 1165)

Jai Ho to all the beings,
Who ain't hypnotized with hate!
Jai Ho to all the beings,
Who ain't living in cavemen days!

Jai Ho to the luchadors,
Who struggle por la igualdad!
Jai Ho to the reformers,
Who value rights over ritual!

Space may be the final frontier,
But heart is the first frontier.
Unless we first conquer the heart,
We'll turn the cosmos into dumpyard.

So I salute, to all explorers of heart!
Jai Ho to the janitors of our cosmic courtyard!

88

# Part 15

## Sonnet 1166

I never studied linguistics,
Yet I became a linguistic enigma.
The sun never studied nuclear fusion,
Yet it is our planet's nuclear messiah.

Some people study poetry,
Some people are poetry.
Some people study nature's forces,
Some people are natural forces.

But being a force of nature means,
bearing ten times more difficulty.
No pain, no lane - no doubt, no clarity.

Servant leaders are force of nature,
Born to add humanness to nature's discourse.
Wake up to your power, and empower the world.
What's the point of power if it crumbles to discord!

Sonnet 1167

## Women in Power
(The Sonnet)


Women in power is power used best,
Men in power means power makes a mess.

For the world to become gender-neutral,
First it's gotta become matriarchal.
Thereafter gender will bear no significance,
Only the capable shall dawn the pedestal.

In patriarchy war and tyranny are the norm,
While peace and equality are exception.
In matriarchy synergy is the norm,
While shallowness is the exception.

Before the world is equalized,
first it's gotta be dehypnotized.
And no world is ever dehypnotized till
the paradigm is mended by the marginalized.

## Sonnet 1168

No world is civilized
till no one is marginal.
All paradigm is prehistoric
till we stop being prejudicial.

Defiance of prejudice is not intolerance,
Intolerance is when prejudice overrides humanity.
Be aware, and never give in to your innate prejudice,
Awareness powered by intention,
puts an end to animosity.

Awareness is not a constant,
awareness is a spectrum.
More you walk the spectrum unrigid,
more insightful and impactful you become.

Rigidity is the greatest impediment to growth -
Never be rigid in any aspect of life.
Don't intellectualize with phrases like growth-mindset -
It is just a living human starting to live alive.

**Part 16**

## Sonnet 1169

Learn to take the self
in and out of the equation.
Be selfless where needed,
be full of yourself when
required by the situation.

Stay docile unless otherwise called for,
Break out as dinosaur when situation demands.
When serving and learning make self nonexistent,
When facing bigots do your narcissistic dance.

Controlled narcissism is a useful faculty,
Put all your faculties to use as life decrees.
Be whole and healthy without ailing allegiances,
Be humble to the helpless, apocalypse to elitists.

Whole human is healthy human,
all others are terminally ill.
Broken mind leads to broken world,
heal the mind and the world will heal.

To heal is to be whole, to be whole is to be healed. For example, before treating a wound, first it's flushed with alcohol to clean the germs. Likewise, to heal this wounded world first we gotta flush the germs of prejudice and discrimination with reason and conscience.

## Sonnet 1170

When the mind is one piece,
there will be peace of mind.
When the earth is one piece,
there will be peace on earth.

Poetry is the way of life in Turkey,
Spirituality is the way of life in India,
Freedom is the way of life in Latam,
Innovation is the way of life in America.

Bring the strongholds of cultures together,
Thus you unlock a paradigm of possibilities.
Past ideologies focus on expansion of fervor,
Waste not this one potent life finding follies.

Live not in denial either - observe all good and bad.
Then do whatever is necessary to lift the world upward.

# Part 17

Political ideologies are not unlike technological inventions - both have expiry dates. Take the first electric bulb for example. When electric filament bulb came into existence it turned gas lamps obsolete - but then power efficient led bulb came into the scene, which turned filament bulbs obsolete. Likewise, back in the days when world conquest was all the craze, nationalism was the fire that united the dominated souls of the invaded lands to stand up to their invaders. But today when the notion of invasion is no longer the norm, and a sense of global oneness is on the rise, nationalism is no longer cool - it is obsolete, inane, and downright prehistoric. Today, it's the fire of integration that lights the world, not tribe, heritage and tradition.

No ideology is ideal, no ideology is ultimate. So, focus on ascension, not allegiance. Evolution is life, rigidity is death - the wheel just keeps turning - monarchy replaced by democracy, democracy replaced by meritocracy - fundamentalism replaced by interfaith, interfaith replaced by freethought - church replaced by state, state replaced by civic duty - capitalism replaced by socialism, socialism replaced by humanitarianism. Countries become cities, cities become neighborhoods, neighborhoods become family - that's real upward mobility - that's civilization.

Civilization is not an heirloom that is left to you, civilization is the keepsake that is left by you. But you can never fathom the sense in this, unless you actually start living as an original sentient human, rather than a dead mouthpiece for your ancestors.

Let me put it to you simply. I am not woke, I am not a feminist, I am not a freethinker - I am just human. I am human, that's why I prioritize rights over ritual - I am human, that's why I value conscience over custom - I am human, that's why I listen to the living rather than the dead.

The problem is, many of the living don't actually live as the living, but as photocopies of the dead - which makes them the walking dead.

# Part 18

## Sonnet 1171

### Kainat Calling
(The Sonnet)


I'll take your leave now,
Kainat is calling -
Ain't gonna stay amidst
your narrowness no more.
You conquered moon,
you'll conquer mars,
yet what's the point,
when your heart is
still beastly sore!
Break your sleep, o drowsy doofus,
Wake up to the auspicious joyville!
Where love and light are supreme law,
Wake up to that valley of joy and zeal!
Everyday is Christmas there,
Everyday is Ramadan and Juneteenth.
Stay in your archaic muck if you like,
I gotta go now, Kainat calling!

**End of Fear**
(Sonnet 1172)


Where the end of fear ends all barrier,
Where biases no longer run amok,
Where end of assumption sets forth ascension,
Where heritage no more wreaks havoc,

Where the head is without bent,
and the heart is never skint,
Where the spine is without dent,
and the eyes are without squint,

Where Christian, Muslim, Sikh 'n Jew,
sit and share a cup of stew,
Where Buddhist, Atheist, Jain, Hindu,
live and laugh as one life crew,

There beyond, where sentience lets no storm to brew,
Out of the fossil, into the fervor, I shall meet you.

Militant atheism is just another intolerance - if you don't get this, you are just as retarded as the religious fundamentalists.

Religious fundamentalism is just another sacrilege - if you don't get this, you are just as infidel as militant atheists.

Intolerance is the enemy, not illogicality. Argumentation without empathy is just hate speech. If someone is doing no harm, then who the hell are you to take away their fantasy! On occasion, healthy fantasy does indeed turn into harmful superstition - at that point it is the duty of every conscientious human to stand up to such superstition. Until then, keep your judgment to yourself.

Evidence-based judgment that undermines human welfare is a violation of human rights, and as such, even evidence becomes inhuman. So, first and foremost, you gotta foster the insight to understand the real-life, humanitarian implications of evidence. You gotta know the kind from unkind, before you know the right from wrong.

Just like memorizing scripture doesn't make you faith police, memorizing facts doesn't make you thought police.

# Part 19

## Sonnet 1173

111

Memorizing scripture doesn't make you religious,
Memorizing facts doesn't make you righteous.
Memorizing the dictionary doesn't make you a poet,
Memorizing law and policy doesn't make you just.

Being right is not the same as being righteous,
Being faithful is not the same as being holy.
Being intelligent is not the same as being wise,
Knowing psychology ain't the same as having empathy.

Evidence based judgment is still judgment,
Scripture based cruelty is still unholy.
Logic driven intolerance is still intolerance,
Heritage driven hate is still inhumanity.

## Sonnet 1174

Nature bred us handicap,
but she also gave us
the prosthetic of mind.
Yet we cling to the handicap
making it our identity,
and refuse all use of mind.

Mind is more than a prosthetic,
Mind holds the supreme might.
Born of nature only mind will
one day conquer nature,
but not till we tame our handicap,
and be the light to our kind.

You call it tradition, I call it slavery -
You call it identity, I call it infection.
Obliterate every last trace of such fanaticism -
Rise above all handicap -
be the herald of your inception!

## Sonnet 1175

If pain delivers sentience,
Give me all the pain of the cosmos!
If tragedy transforms animal to human,
Let all tragedy befall my shoulders!

If darkness makes the sun bright,
Let my life stay engulfed in ominosity.
Let the world know me from my triumphs,
While I know myself from my tragedies.

Study my words, you'll find my wholeness -
Penetrate the words, you'll find emptiness.
Without knowing emptiness, wholeness is empty -
Wholeness dawns when you realize nonexistence.

Nonexistence is the beginning of existence.
Awareness of nothingness is the birth of sentience.

Part 20

## Sonnet 1176

When you are nothing,
you are everything.
When you stop mimicking,
you start living.

Sing to the world,
like birds sing to the sky -
Hug the world like rain hugs the earth.
Course through the alleys,
like wind courses through leaves -
Kiss the world like the sun kisses the earth.

Loosen all knots of ancient nuttery,
Live up to the original call of life.
Lay your head at the feet of the soil,
Listen inward to the gospel of light.

Let all pride be drowned in the depth of tears,
Let all pomp be crushed by the load of pain.
Let all counterfeit self become distant memory,
Let life be identified by your one chosen lane.

## Sonnet 1177

Let the lane course through your vein,
Let your mission invade every pore.
Develop in your mind a bird-like compass,
Let your eyes see past the unopened door.

You are the source of all your fortune,
You are the root of your destiny.
Never compromise integrity for support -
Honest struggle is beautiful,
dishonest success ugly.

A greedy world raises greedy children,
Focused on wallets not backbone.
Once you compromise, it becomes a habit,
Furthermore it keeps humanity unhoned.

Backbone compromised is backbone vilified -
Be the explorer of life, love and liberty,
rather than pampering prehistoric insecurity.

## Sonnet 1178

Five little rich tourists sink in a sub,
Wallets open without limit on a search-n-rescue op.
A 1000 migrants die each year tryna cross the sea,
Borders tighten in sheer fear with no show of mercy.

People are only worth saving
if their savings is super healthy.
50 Shades would be a Hitchcock film
if the sicko had no money.

Empathy is a far cry, life is never the issue.
While next-door-neighbor cries of hunger,
Netflix wets more tissue.

# Part 21

## Sonnet 1179

Time and again it's proven,
all lives do not matter.
How could this be a human world,
it's just a glorified disaster!

Ukraine is worth aiding, but not Afghanistan,
Tourists are worth saving, but not refugees.
Loss of any life is indeed a moment of tragedy,
Then why this double-standard and hypocrisy!

To err is animal, to correct is human -
Animals stay animal because their
neural capacity for correction is limited.
If humans behave animal justifying error
rather than eagerly correcting them,
what's the point of having a brain so potent!

There is no gentle soul, there is no wise -
Within every human there's a savage animal soul.
Question is, are you willing to humanize yourself,
Are you willing to let your conscience roll!

People boast about having a gentle soul. I'll tell you right away, I am not gentle, I am the pinnacle of everything that is violent in nature. Yet nobody has ever seen me violent - you know why? Because gentleness is not the absence of violence, gentleness is the mastery over violence. Or to put it another way - nonviolence is not the absence of violence, nonviolence is the mastery over violence.

Self mastery is the greatest mastery,
Where the master is you, and pupil is you.
Self conquered is world conquered,
Because you are the world, the world is you.

Get to know the animal within,
World will know the human outside.
Resist no more the darkness within,
World will wake up to a dawn divine.

Kendini iyi tanı be insan,
Sonra dünya seni tanıyacak!
Kendine güven be insan,
Sonra dünya sana güvenecek!

İçindeki canavarı tanı be insan,
Sonra dünya bir insanı tanıyacak!
İçindeki karanlığı tanı be insan,
İlahi bir güneş dünyada doğacak!

Conquista tu animal interior,
El mundo obtendrá un verdadero humano.
Ser amigo de la oscuridad interior,
El mundo será testigo de un amanecer divino.

# Part 22

## Sonnet 1180

Strum on heartstrings the song of synergy,
Be the headstrong harbinger of harmony.
Coexistence is existence when human is whole,
Wake up to duty, geopolitics will be history.

Awake, arise and shoulder the world -
To live life is to answer duty's call.
Duty is the better name of existence -
Dutybound we rise, dutyfree we fall.

Life begins with accountability,
Heart begins with shared liberty.
Shared liberty is civil liberty,
Uneven liberty is jungle liberty.

Liberation is the by-product,
Accountability is the cause.
All peace will come down pouring,
Once accountable in a mindful pause.

## Sonnet 1181

Mind can never be empty of thoughts,
Mind without thought is a mindless lie.
Don't force the mind to be empty of thought,
Focus instead on fostering a thoughtful mind.

Trash all archaic lies disguised as wisdom,
Learn to penetrate the myths of mysticism.
Self-correction is world-correction,
You are the root of all social correction.

World is the mirror,
Mind is the light.
When the mind is all dusty,
There is only night.

Awareness is the beginning of consciousness,
Awareness is the beginning of civilization.
Intolerance is but the absence of awareness -
Awareness not of survival, but of illumination.

# Justice Beyond Month
### (Sonnet 1182)

Pride that ends with the end of June,
is but an episode of looney tunes.
Divergence that dies with April's wake,
is no inclusion but bark of buffoons.

Black history that ends with the end of February,
is not solidarity but a hashtag cacophony.
Women's history that ends with the end of March,
is no celebration but a sacrilege of equality.

When AAPI are only visible in the month of May,
It ain't no visibility but a mockery of life.
When nativeness is welcome till October 15th,
It ain't integration but desecration of light.

Awareness is justice when it reduces prejudice.
But one that's trendy only in specific months,
is no awareness but a different kind of malice.

Acceptance is awareness, awareness is life.
100 calendars fall short to celebrate mindlight.

**Part 23**

## Sonnet 1183

Don't sync your heartbeats
to the drumbeats of war.
Strum the chords of coexistence
on the frets of fervor.

Acceptance is awareness,
awareness civilization.
Expansion is cosmic lift,
exclusion castration.

Division is everywhere,
Inclusion under attack.
Morning sun is like antiseptic,
to the germs of hate and hurt.

Submit to no night,
for light is not normal.
In a world rooted in injustice,
justice is always abnormal.

## Sonnet 1184

You've ushered me with a lot of titles -
genius, gifted, awakened, and what not!
But only adjective I'm interested in,
is "Impossible", and nothing short.

I am but a drunken treasure,
with neither beginning nor end.
Don't fall prey to gatekeepers -
I am the valley, you are my gate.

You are the gate, you are the keeper,
All cultish claims are null and void.
Don't go chasing second-hand analysis,
Sail forth boldly on a first-hand voyage.

In a world that rewards second-hand existence,
Stand alone and original, as a first-hand sapiens.

First duty of a first-hand sapiens is to stand their
ground of their original humanness, no matter
how much the paradigm peddles cruelty and
persecution as signs of either sanctity or sanity.
The next sonnet will demonstrate further.

## Hijab and Habit
(Sonnet 1185)

Hijab and Habit are both
symbols of sacred humility,
Yet the latter receives respect,
while the former faces cruelty.

Christ is a revered figure to the muslims,
Yet muslims are frowned upon by christians.
Most christians are plain unchristian,
They are the cause of Christ's crucifixion.

In the world of animal holiness,
Crucifixion continues in different form.
Bigotry once killed a vessel of love,
His pupils continue the hate and harm.

I have zero tolerance for intolerance,
whether from intellectual atheists
or mindless fundamentalists.
Facts and faith both gotta earn admittance,
by causing not crippling humane uplift.

Part 24

## Sonnet 1186

It's useless to know all the facts,
If you don't understand human frailty.
It's useless to memorize some holy books,
If your heart lacks basic inclusivity.

Facts and faith both are useless on their own,
How you practice them defines their worth.
If all they do is turn you bitter and cynical,
You know no reason, you know no religion,
with cranium and chest a vacant lot.

Some people have a vacant lot for a brain,
Some people have a vacant lot for a heart.
Some people's mind has full-on vacancy,
Some people's vacancy is in spinal cord.

Only way to remove all of life's vacancy,
is to live life rooted in universality.

Life rooted in universality,
Mind rooted in curiosity,
Heart rooted in equality,
Spine rooted in integrity -

Or simpler yet -

Life rooted in mind,
Mind rooted in spine,
Spine rooted in heart,
Heart rooted in kind -

That's how civilization unfolds,
That's how human existence unfolds.

## Sonnet 1187

All are born to live in society,
Very few make the society live.
All take up space on the fabric of world,
Very few make space for the world to live.

All are born as part of society,
Very few have society as part of them.
All are born in the tick of time,
Very few give a tick to make time humane.

Time is an intriguing construct,
It exists so long exists the mind.
Its morality is rooted in mind,
Its destiny dictated by mind.

I am time, you are time -
We are the vessel, and the vanguard.
What we decide goes -
We are the voice, we are the victor.

**Part 25**

## Sonnet 1188

1147

Togetherness is not a destination,
Togetherness is the journey.
Inclusion is not intelligence,
Inclusion is sanity.

More you intellectualize life,
Life loses its sweetness.
More you fantasize about life,
Life loses its truthfulness.

Little facts, little fiction -
That's the secret to a good life.
Maintain your lean as it appeals,
But never let the lean overwhelm life.

The grand picture of life lies in the little moments,
which the intellectual never finds, nor the superstitious.
Grand picture of life dawns upon the life lived grand,
It unfolds on its own once you're no more a tribal dunce.

## Sonnet 1189

Grand picture brings grand responsibility -
Better yet, when you are responsible
you see the grand picture.
But the grand picture is far from serene,
It only keeps  you ever-awake for disaster.

Our mess, our mend -
let the privileged apes scarper.
Those who are humans must stand unbent,
For we the world's caretaker.

*I don't know about Mars and Moon,
On my planet I am brakeless loon.
Exploiting dreams and hope,
when chimpanzees elope,
I stand grounded as an unbent boon.

Thus speaks human, without abandoning duty.
Life without duty is the beginning of indignity.




*This third stanza of the sonnet is a limerick -
Naskar Limerick 1.

## Sonnet 1190

Accountability brings dignity,
Dignity further empowers accountability.
Accountability keeps you awake day and night,
Makes you restless till you bring felicity.

Restless and sleepless, yet facing ruthlessness,
Thus the reformer brings forth rejuvenation.
Every night brings torment, every day is disaster,
Yet the reformer never gives in to desperation.

**Ominous though the night bring fright,
Disastrous though the day might strike.
Hand on chest,
with spine unbent,
Reformer walks as ray of right.

Be the ray, without delay -
You are the hope for all humanity.
You know what the word "hope" means -
HOPE means Human On Patrol Eternally.

**Limerick 2

## Sonnet 1191

You ask me, how do you do that,
How do you take society on shoulders?
Question is, where did you learn indifference -
Discard indifference, and the path appears!

The path is already there in you,
Indifference and apathy make you blind.
Then you flutter here and there,
chasing one fool after another,
Till you realize your self-imposed fright.

***Birds don't learn to fly, they just do.
I didn't learn to write, I just do.
Stop grovelling to authority,
embolden your curiosity,
All the answers lie dormant in you.

Bow before gentle expertise, not authority,
Respect those who are worthy of respect.
Stature doesn't entitle one to nothing,
Excellence and gentleness combined
make one worthy of respect.

***Limerick 3

# Part 26

## Sonnet 1192

Take off your clothes and post a selfie,
A million animals will shower you attention.
But cover up all and open your heart,
Only precious few humans will care to listen.

Don't confuse attention with care,
Those who care might not follow you.
But you can be sure of one little thing,
99% of your followers don't care about you.

****Break your addiction of likes and share,
Outgrow the lure of all golden snare.
Focus on your walk,
not on outside talk,
Sun's glow always makes the vermin glare.

Exposure has become a mark of growth,
Such is the muck the world takes as normal!
In such norm, you gotta be an anomaly,
Only then shall you rise a figure universal.

****Limerick 4

## Sonnet 1193

Being a public figure and a figure
to the public, are two difference things.
Public figure thrives on attention,
figure to the public thrives on accountability.

Credit craving public figures
are rampant in every corner.
Accountable public servants
are scarce and getting scarcer.

Be a public servant,
not a public figure.
Be a mindful inspirer,
not a mindless entertainer.

Be the public, better the public,
by working for, not under, society.
Lift up the world on your shoulder,
practicing conscience, not conformity.

## Sonnet 1194

It's easy to be a public figure,
not so much to be a public servant.
It's easy to draw attention,
not so much to reform mindset.

Heart, brain and backbone,
if you have these three,
you have everything to succeed,
you can reshape all of humanity.

Yesterday I was stupid,
I wanted to change the world.
Today I am stupider still,
So I am changing the world.

Your life is the change,
Live it as a declaration!
When all are busy making excuses,
Take charge as a living reformation.

When brain stops,
When heart stops,
What is left of you?

When eyes fail,
When memory fails,
What is left of you?

When your last molecule
has merged with nature,
What is left of you?

That's what you've really achieved -
Testament to the fact that,
there ever was a you.

# BIBLIOGRAPHY

Archer M., (2000), Being Human: The Problem of Agency. Cambridge University Press.

Adolphs R (2003) Cognitive neuroscience of human social behaviour. Nature Rev Neurosci 4: 165–178.

Adolphs R, Tranel D, Damasio AR (2003) Dissociable neural systems for recognizing emotions. Brain Cogn 52: 61–69.

Andresen, Jensine, and Robert Forman, eds. Cognitive Models and Spiritual Maps. Bowling Green, Ohio: Imprint Academic, 2000.

Bernstein R.J., (1971), Praxis and Action: Contemporary Philosophies of Human Activity. Philadelphia: University of Pennsylvania Press.

Bernstein R.J., (1976), The Restructuring Social and Political Thought.

Bogen, J.E.(1995a), 'On the neurophysiology of consciousness: Part I. An overview', Consciousness and Cognition, 4.

Bogen, J.E. (1995b), 'On the neurophysiology of consciousness: Part II. Constraining the semantic problem', Consciousness and Cognition, 4.

Bremner, J. D., R. Soufer, et al. (2001). "Gender differences in cognitive and neural correlates of remembrance of emotional words." Psychopharmacol Bull 35 (3).

Brothers, L. (2002). The social brain: A project for integrating primate behavior and neurophysiology in a new domain. In J. T. Cacioppo et al. (Eds.), Foundations in neuroscience. Cambridge, MA: MIT Press.

Buss, D. D. (2003). Evolutionary Psychology: The New Science of Mind, 2nd ed. New York: Allyn & Bacon.

Buss, D. M. (1989). "Conflict between the sexes: Strategic interference and the evocation of anger and upset." J Pers Soc Psychol 56 (5).

Buss, D. M. (1995). "Psychological sex differences. Origins through sexual selection." Am Psychol 50 (3).

Buss, D. M., and D. P. Schmitt (1993). "Sexual strategies theory: An evolutionary perspective on human mating." Psychol Rev 100 (2).

Chomsky Noam, (2016) Who Rules the World?

Churchland, P.S. (1986), Neurophilosophy (Cambridge, MA: The MIT Press).

Churchland, P.S. & Ramachandran, V.S. (1993), 'Filling in: Why Dennett is wrong', in Dennett and His Critics:

Demystifying Mind, ed. B. Dahlbom (Oxford: Blackwell Scientific Press).

Churchland, P.S., Ramachandran, V.S. & Sejnowski, T.J. (1994), 'A critique of pure vision', in Large- scale Neuronal Theories of the Brain, ed. C. Koch & J.L. Davis (Cambridge, MA: The MIT Press).

Crick, F. (1994), The Astonishing Hypothesis: The Scientific Search for the Soul (New York: Simon and Schuster).

Crick, F. (1996), 'Visual perception: rivalry and consciousness', Nature, 379.

Crick, F. & Koch, C. (1992), 'The problem of consciousness', Scientific American, 267.

d'Aquili, Eugene. "Senses of Reality in Science and Religion." Zygon 17, no 4 (1982)

d'Aquili, Eugene. "The Biopsychological Determinants of Religious Ritual Behavior." Zygon 10, no. 1 (1975)

d'Aquili, Eugene. "The Myth-Ritual Complex: A Biogenetic Structural Analysis." Zygon 18, no. 3 (1983)

d'Aquili, Eugene, and Andrew Newberg. The Mystical Mind: Probing the Biology of Religious Experience. Minneapolis: Fortress Press, 1999.

Damasio, A. (1994) Descartes' Error: Emotion, Reason and the Human Brain. New York, Putnams.

Damasio, A. (1999) The Feeling of What Happens: Body, Emotion and the Making of Consciousness. London, Heinemann.

Darwin, C. (1859) On the Origin of Species by Means of Natural Selection. London, Murray.

Darwin, C. (1871) The Descent of Man and Selection in Relation to Sex. London, John Murray.

Dawkins, R. (1976) The Selfish Gene. Oxford, Oxford University Press; a new edition, with additional material, was published in 1989.

Dewhurst, Kenneth, and A. W. Beard. "Sudden Religious Conversions in Temporal Lobe Epilepsy." British Journal of Psychiatry 117 (1970)

Dewhurst K, Beard AW. Sudden religious conversions in temporal lobe epilepsy. 1970 Epilepsy Behav 2003

Devinsky O, Lai G. Spirituality and religion in epilepsy. Epilepsy Behav 2008.

E. Horvitz, "One Hundred Year Study on Artificial Intelligence: Reflections and Framing," ed: Stanford University, 2014.

Eckhart Meister, Selected Writings

Farah, M.J. (1989), 'The neural basis of mental imagery', Trends in Neurosciences, 10.

Freud, S. "Selected papers on hysteria and other psychoneuroses" Journal of Nervous and Mental Disease 1909.

Freud, S. "The Origin and Development of Psychoanalysis", 1910

Freud, S. "Psychopathology of everyday life", 1914

Freud, S. "Beyond the Pleasure Principle", 1920

Frith, C.D. & Dolan, R.J. (1997), 'Abnormal beliefs: Delusions and memory', Paper presented at the May, 1997, Harvard Conference on Memory and Belief.

Gay, Volney, ed. Neuroscience and Religion. Plymouth, UK: Lexington Books, 2009.

Gazzaniga, M. S. (1985). The social brain. New York: Basic Books.

Gazzaniga, M.S. (1993), 'Brain mechanisms and conscious experience', Ciba Foundation Symposium, 174.

Geschwind N. "Behavioural changes in temporal lobe epilepsy". Psychol Med. 1979.

Gellhorn, E., Kiely, W.F. "Mystical states of consciousness: neurophysiological and clinical aspects." J Nerv Ment Dis. 1972;154:399-405.

Gilbert SL, Dobyns WB, Lahn BT (2005) Genetic links between brain development and brain evolution. Nat Rev Genet 6.

Gray JA. The Psychology of Fear and Stress. 2nd ed. New York, NY: Cambridge University Press; 1988.

Gloor, P. (1992), 'Amygdala and temporal lobe epilepsy', in The Amygdala: Neurobiological Aspects of Emotion, Memory and Mental

Dysfunction, ed J.P. Aggleton (New York: Wiley-Liss).

Gross CG, Rocha-Miranda CE, Bender DB (1972) Visual properties of neurons in the inferotemporal cortex of the macaque. J Neurophysiol 35: 96–111.

Guevara Che, The Motorcycle Diaries, 1992

Hardy, G. H. (1940). Ramanujan. Cambridge: Cambridge University Press.

Hall, Daniel, Keith Meador, and Harold Koenig. "Measuring Religiousness in Health Research: Review and Critique." Journal of Religion and Health 47, no. 2 (2008)

Harris, Sam, Jonas Kaplan, Ashley Curiel, Susan Bookheimer, Marco Iacoboni, and Mark Cohen. "The Neural Correlates of Religious and Nonreligious Belief." PLoS One 4, no. 10 (October 1, 2009)

Halgren, E. (1992), 'Emotional neurophysiology of the amygdala within the context of human cognition', in The Amygdala: Neurobiological Aspects of Emotion, Memory and Mental Dysfunction, ed J.P. Aggleton (New York: Wiley-Liss).

Halligan PW, Fink GR, Marshal JC, Vallar G. 2003. Spatial cognition: evidence from visual neglect. Trends Cogn Sci.

Handbook of Emotions, Edited by Michael Lewis, Jeannette M. Haviland-Jones, and Lisa Feldman Barrett, The Guilford Press; 3rd edition (2010).

Hameroff, S.R. and Penrose, R. (1996) Conscious events as orchestrated space-time selections. Journal of Consciousness Studies 3(1), 36-53; also reprinted in J. Shear (ed.) (1997) Explaining Consciousness-The Hard Problem. Cambridge, MA, MIT Press, 177-95.

Harding, D.E. (1961) On Having no Head: Zen and the Re-Discovery of the Obvious. London, Buddhist Society.

Hardy, A. (1979) The Spiritual Nature of Man: A Study of Contemporary Religious Experience. Oxford, Clarendon Press.

Harre, R. and Gillett, G. (1994) The Discursive Mind. Thousand Oaks, CA, Sage.

Haugeland, J. (ed.) (1997) Mind Design II: Philosophy, Psychology, Artificial Intelligence. Cambridge, MA, MIT Press.

Hauser, M.D. (2000) Wild Minds: What Animals Really Think. New York, Henry Holt and Co.; London, Penguin.

Hilgard, E.R. (1986) Divided Consciousness: Multiple Controls in Human Thought and Action. New York, Wiley.

Hilton, E.N., Lundberg, T.R. Transgender Women in the Female Category of Sport: Perspectives on Testosterone Suppression and Performance Advantage. Sports Med 51, 199–214 (2021).

Hitler, Adolf. Mein Kampf, 1925

Hodgson, R. (1891) A case of double consciousness. Proceedings of the Society for Psychical Research 7, 221-58.

Hofstadter, D.R. and Dennett, D.C. (eds) (1981) The Mind's I: Fantasies and Reflections on Self and Soul. London, Penguin.

Holland, J. (ed.) (2001) Ecstasy: The Complete Guide: A Comprehensive Look at the Risks and Benefits of MDMA. Rochester, VT, Park Street Press.

Holmes, D.S. (1987) The influence of meditation versus rest on physiological arousal. In M. West (ed.)

The Psychology of Meditation. Oxford, Clarendon Press, 81-103.

Holmstrom, David. 1992, Christian Science Monitor

Holloway RL (1996) Evolution of the human brain. In: Lock A, Peters CR (eds) Handbook of human symbolic evolution. Oxford University Press, Oxford

Jeannerod M (1988) The neural and behavioural organization of goal-directed movements. Clarendon Press, Oxford.

Johnson-Frey SH, Maloof FR, Newman-Norlund R, Farrer C, Inati S, Grafton ST (2003) Actions or hand-objects interactions? Human inferior frontal cortex and action observation. Neuron 39: 1053–1058.

Jackson, F. (1982) Epiphenomenal qualia. Philosophical Quarterly 32, 127-36.

James, W. (1890) The Principles of Psychology (2 volumes). London, Macmillan.

James, W. (1902) The Varieties of Religious Experience: A Study in Human Nature. New York and London, Longmans, Green and Co.

Jansen, K. (2001) Ketamine: Dreams and Realities. Sarasota, FL, Multidisciplinary Association for Psychedelic Studies.

Jay, M. (ed.) (1999) Artificial Paradises: A Drugs Reader. London, Penguin.

Jaynes, J. (1976) The Origin of Consciousness in the Breakdown of the Bicameral Mind. New York, Houghton Mifflin.

Kandel, E. R. In Search of Memory: The Emergence of a New Science of Mind, W. W. Norton & Company (2007).

Kandel E. R. Schwartz JH, Jessel TM. Principles of neural sciences. New York; McGraw Hill, 2000.

Kanwisher, N. (2001) Neural events and perceptual awareness. Cognition 79, 89-113; also reprinted inS. Dehaene (ed.) The Cognitive Neuroscience of Consciousness. Cambridge, MA, MIT Press, 89-113.

Kihlstrom, J.F. (1996) Perception without awareness of what is perceived, learning without awareness of what is learned. In M. Velmans (ed.) The Science of Consciousness. London, Routledge, 23-46.

Kosslyn, S.M. (1980) Image and Mind. Cambridge, MA, Harvard University Press.

Kosslyn, S.M. (1988) Aspects of a cognitive neuroscience of mental imagery. Science 240, 1621-6.

Kjaer, Troels, Camilla Bertelsen, Paola Piccini, David Brooks, Jorgen Alving, and Hans Lou. "Increased Dopamine Tone during Meditation- Induced Change of Consciousness." Cognitive Brain Research 13, no. 2 (April 2002)

Kölmel HW. 1985. Complex visual hallucinations in the hemianopic field. J Neurol Neurosurg Psychiatry.

Koenig, Harold. "Research on Religion, Spirituality, and Mental Health: A Review." Canadian Journal of Psychiatry 54, no. 5 (May 2009)

Koenig, Harold, ed. Handbook of Religion and Mental Health. San Diego, CA: Academic Press, 1998

Kraepelin E. Psychiatry: A Textbook for Students and Physicians. New York, NY: Science History Publications; 1990.

Lauglin, Charles, John McManus, and Eugene d'Aquili. Brain, Symbol, and Experience. 2nd ed. New York: Columbia University Press, 1992

Lakoff, G. and M. Johnson (1999). Philosophy in the flesh. Basic Books: New York.

LeDoux, J. E. (1996). The emotional brain. New York: Simon & Schuster.

LeDoux, J.E. (1992), 'Emotion and the amygdala', in The Amygdala: Neurobiological Aspects of Emo- tion, Memory and Mental Dysfunction, ed J.P. Aggleton (New York: Wiley-Liss).

Levin, D.T. and Simons, D.J. (1997) Failure to detect changes to attended objects in motion pictures. Psychonomic Bulletin and Review 4, 501-6.

Levine,J. (1983) Materialism and qualia: the explanatory gap. Pacific Philosophical Quarterly 64, 354-61.

Levine,J. (2001) Purple Haze: The Puzzle of Consciousness. New York, Oxford University Press. Levine, S. (1979) A Gradual Awakening. New York, Doubleday.

Levinson, B.W. (1965) States of awareness during general anaesthesia. British Journal of Anaesthesia 37, 544-6.

Lewicki, P., Czyzewska, M. and Hoffman, H. (1987) Unconscious acquisition of complex procedural knowledge. Journal of Experimental Psychology: Learning, Memory and Cognition 13, 523-30.

Naskar, Abhijit. "What is Mind?", 2016

Naskar, Abhijit. "Love, God & Neurons: Memoir of A Scientist who found himself by getting lost", 2016

Naskar, Abhijit. "Principia Humanitas", 2017

Naskar, Abhijit. "We Are All Black: A Treatise on Racism", 2017

Naskar, Abhijit. "Either Civilized or Phobic: A Treatise on Homosexuality", 2017

Naskar, Abhijit. "Build Bridges not Walls: In the name of Americana", 2018

Naskar, Abhijit. "Citizens of Peace: Beyond the Savagery of Sovereignty", 2019

Naskar, Abhijit. "The Constitution of The United Peoples of Earth", 2019

Naskar, Abhijit. "Mission Reality", 2019

Naskar, Abhijit. "Good Scientist: When Science and Service Combine", 2020

Newberg, Andrew, and Jeremy Iversen. "The Neural Basis of the Complex Mental Task of Meditation: Neurotransmitter and Neurochemical Considerations." Medical Hypotheses 61, no. 2 (2003).

Newberg, Andrew. "How God Changes Your Brain: An Introduction to Jewish Neurotheology", CCAR

Journal: The Reform Jewish Quarterly, Winter 2016.

Newberg, Andrew, and Stephanie Newberg. "A Neuropsychological Perspective on Spiritual Development." In Handbook of Spiritual Development in Childhood and Adolescence, edited by Eugene Roehlkepartain, Pamela King, Linda Wagener, and Peter Benson. London: Sage Publications, Inc., 2005

Newberg, Andrew. "The Neurotheology Link An Intersection Between Spirituality and Health", Alternative and Complimentary Therapies, Vol 21 No 1, February 2015.

Newberg, Andrew, Nancy Wintering, Dharma Khalsa, Hannah Roggenkamp, and Mark Waldman. "Meditation Effects on Cognitive Function and Cerebral Blood Flow in Subjects with Memory Loss: A Preliminary Study." Journal of Alzheimer's Disease 20, no. 2 (2010)

Nash, M. (1995), 'Glimpses of the mind', Time.

Nesse RM. Proximate and evolutionary studies of anxiety, stress and depression: synergy at the interface. Neurosci Biobehav Rev. 1999;23:895-903.

Nicolelis, Miguel. (2011) "Beyond Boundaries: The New Neuroscience of Connecting Brains with Machines--- and How It Will Change Our Lives", Times Books

O'Hara, K. and Scutt, T. (1996) There is no hard problem of consciousness. Journal of Consciousness Studies 3(4), 290-302, reprinted in J. Shear (ed.) (1997) Explaining Consciousness. Cambridge, MA, MIT Press, 69-82.

O'Regan, J.K. and Noe, A. (2001) A sensorimotor account of vision and visual consciousness. Behavioral and Brain Sciences 24(5), 883-917.

Ornstein, R.E. (1977) The Psychology of Consciousness (2nd edn). New York, Harcourt.

Ornstein, R.E. (1986) The Psychology of Consciousness (3rd edn). New York, Pehguin.

Ornstein, R.E. (1992) The Evolution of Consciousness. New York, Touchstone.

Penfield W, Faulk ME (1955) The insula: further observations on its function. Brain 78: 445– 470.

Penrose, R. (1994), Shadows of the Mind (Oxford: Oxford University Press).

Penrose, R. (1989), The Emperor's New Mind: Concerning Computers, Minds and The Laws of Physics (Oxford: Oxford University Press).

Persinger, "'I would kill in God's name' role of sex, weekly church attendance, report of a religious experience and limbic lability" Perceptual and Motor Skills 1997.

Persinger "Experimental simulation of the God experience" Neurotheology 2003.

Persinger, Corradini, Clement, Keaney, et al "Neurotheology and its convergence with neuroquantology" NeuroQuantology 2010.

Persinger. "The neuropsychiatry of paranormal experiences". J Neuropsychiatry Clin Neurosci 2001.

Persinger. "Neuropsychological bases of god beliefs", New York: Praeger, 1987

Persinger. "Temporal lobe epileptic signs and correlative behaviors displayed by normal populations", Journal of General Psychology, 1986

Perry BD, Pollard R. Homeostasis, stress, trauma, and adaptation. A neurodevelopmental view of childhood trauma. Child Adolesc Psychiatr Clin N Am. 1998;7:33.

Ramachandran VS. Behavioral and magnetoencephalographic correlates of plasticity in the adult human brain. Proc Natl Acad Sci USA 1993; 90: 10413–20.

Ramachandran VS. Plasticity and functional recovery in neurology. Clin Med 2005; 5: 368–73.

Rock I, Victor J. Vision and touch: an experimentally created conflict between the two senses. Science 1964; 143: 594–6.

Roberts, TA; Smalley, J; Ahrendt, D (December 2020). "Effect of gender affirming hormones on athletic performance in transwomen and transmen: implications for sporting organisations and legislators". British Journal of Sports Medicine. 55 (11): 577–583

Royet JP, Plailly J, Delon-Martin C, Kareken DA, Segebarth C (2003) fMRI of emotional responses to odors: influence of hedonic valence and judgment, handedness, and gender. Neuroimage 20: 713–728.

Rozin R Haidt J and McCauley CR (2000) Disgust. In: Lewis M, Haviland-Jones JM (eds) Handbook of Emotion. 2nd Edition. Guilford Press, New York, pp 637–653.

Saxe R, Carey S, Kanwisher N (2004) Understanding other minds: linking developmental psychology and functional neuroimaging. Annu Rev Psychol 55: 87–124.

S. J. Russell and P. Norvig, Artificial intelligence: a modern approach (3rd edition): Prentice Hall, 2009.

Singer T, Seymour B, O'Doherty J, Kaube H, Dolan RJ, Frith CD (2004) Empathy for pain involves the affective but not the sensory components of pain. Science 303: 1157–1162.

Smith A (1759) The theory of moral sentiments (ed. 1976). Clarendon Press, Oxford.

Schilling, Vincent. 2017, indian country today

Stein, Stephen K. 2017, The Sea in World History: Exploration, Travel, and Trade

Tesla N. "My Inventions", 1919

T. R. Society, "Machine learning: the power and promise of computers that learn by example," ed. The Royal Society, 2017.

Tomasello M, Call J (1997) Primate cognition. Oxford University Press, Oxford

186